Landmark Events in American History

The Atom Bomb Project

Dale Anderson

WORLD ALMANAC® LIBRARY

Please visit our web site at: www.worldalmanaclibrary.com
For a free color catalog describing World Almanac® Library's list of high-quality
books and multimedia programs, call 1-800-848-2928 (USA) or 1-800-387-3178
(Canada). World Almanac® Library's fax: (414) 332-3567.

Library of Congress Cataloging-in-Publication Data

Anderson, Dale, 1953-
    The atom bomb project / by Dale Anderson.
      p. cm. — (Landmark events in American history)
    Includes bibliographical references and index.
    ISBN 0-8368-5385-7 (lib. bdg.)
    ISBN 0-8368-5413-6 (softcover)
    1. Atomic bomb—United States—History—Juvenile literature. 2. Manhattan
Project (U.S.)—History—Juvenile literature. [1. Atomic bomb—History.
2. Manhattan Project (U.S.).] I. Title. II. Series.
    QC773.3.U5A56   2004
    355.8'25119'097309044—dc22   2003064579

First published in 2004 by
World Almanac® Library
330 West Olive Street, Suite 100
Milwaukee, WI 53212 USA

Copyright © 2004 by World Almanac® Library.

Produced by Discovery Books
Editor: Sabrina Crewe
Designer and page production: Sabine Beaupré
Photo researcher: Sabrina Crewe
Maps and diagrams: Stefan Chabluk
World Almanac® Library editorial direction: Mark J. Sachner
World Almanac® Library art direction: Tammy Gruenewald
World Almanac® Library production: Jessica Morris

Photo credits: AP/Wide World Photos: pp. 11, 13, 15, 20, 32, 38, 39, 41;
Corbis: pp. 5, 6, 7, 8, 9, 10, 16, 17, 18, 21, 25, 26, 28, 29, 30, 31, 42; White
Sands Missile Range: cover, pp. 4, 19, 22, 23, 27, 33, 34, 35, 36, 37, 40, 43.

Printed in the United States of America

1 2 3 4 5 6 7 8 9 08 07 06 05 04

Contents

Introduction

The Destroyer of Worlds

"We waited until the blast had passed, walked out of the shelter and then it was extremely solemn. We knew the world would not be the same. A few people laughed, a few people cried. Most people were silent. I remembered the line from the Hindu scripture . . . 'Now I am become Death, the destroyer of worlds.' I suppose we all thought that, one way or another."

J. Robert Oppenheimer, director of the Manhattan Project, recalling the atomic bomb test in July 1945

Nuclear Energy

In the early and mid-1900s, a series of scientific discoveries changed the world by giving humans the ability to produce **nuclear energy**. This power brought with it great potential and also great danger. In the United States on July 16, 1945, an **atomic** bomb was tested that used nuclear energy to create a devastating and deadly explosion. The successful test changed the course of warfare forever and introduced a threat that people have lived with ever since.

Top Secret

The test of the world's first atomic bomb was the result of a long effort carried out by the United States during World War II. This work—the Manhattan Project—involved scores of scientists, hundreds of military men, and thousands of

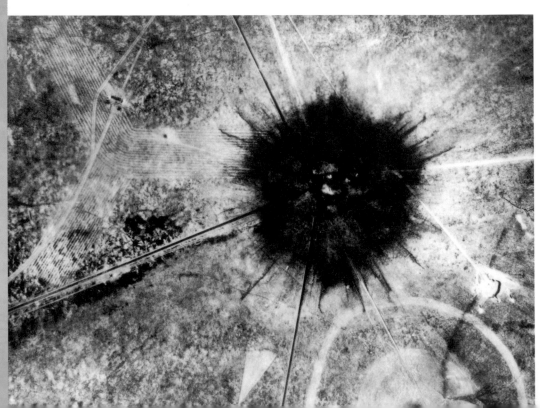

The first atomic bomb test took place in a remote desert in New Mexico. This aerial photograph shows the site about twenty-four hours after the test explosion.

The first atomic bomb ever used in warfare was dropped on the Japanese city of Hiroshima on August 6, 1945. This was the result.

workers across the country. It took several years to complete. Despite the size and scale of this project, it was so secret that even the vice president of the United States did not know about it. The secrecy was needed because the project's leaders feared what would happen if the United States' enemies gained knowledge of this destructive new weapon.

Using the Bomb

In the end, it was the United States and not its enemies that used the atomic bomb. Less than a month after the successful test in 1945, two atomic bombs were dropped on Japanese cities by U.S. airplanes, causing thousands of deaths and mass destruction. The Japanese surrendered within days, and World War II came to an end.

Civilian Deaths

Well over 100,000 people were killed when the atomic bombs were dropped, and thousands more would die later because of their impact. Although the number of deaths caused by the atomic bombs is horrifying, it was only a small fraction of the total **civilian** casualties in World War II. By the time the war ended, about 20 million civilians had died. The **Soviet Union**, with 7 million deaths, and Poland, with nearly 6 million civilian deaths, suffered the most. The brutal actions of German forces account for the high number of deaths in those countries. Bombing from the air killed about 800,000 German civilians and about 700,000 Japanese civilians.

Chapter 1

A World at War

Adolf Hitler of Germany (left) and Benito Mussolini of Italy (behind Hitler) in Germany in 1940. Hitler and Mussolini were dictators in their own nations, and both wanted to extend their power to control other countries, too.

The Rise of the Dictators

In the 1920s and 1930s, many countries were in turmoil. They had been weakened first by the destruction of World War I and then by a major **depression**. Millions of people were out of work and hungry. Many joined extreme political parties, led by men who promised easy solutions to their countries' problems.

Two of these leaders in Europe were **fascists**. The first to arise was Benito Mussolini, who took power in Italy in the 1920s. He pushed through laws that gave him great control and took away people's freedoms. Adolf Hitler used similar tactics in Germany: his Nazi Party included highly disciplined, uniformed troops who used violence against any opponents. Meanwhile, Hitler gave powerful speeches promising a better future. After the 1933 elections, Hitler became a dictator with complete control of the country.

In the Soviet Union, Josef Stalin, a **communist**, seized power. He squashed all rivals, executing many and throwing others into prison for life. His policies transformed Soviet society and resulted in the deaths of millions of people. Stalin built a strong secret police force that cracked down on all opponents.

In Japan, top military leaders managed to gain power over the country's civilian government. These leaders wanted the country to move aggressively against its neighbors. Only by seizing more land, they said, could Japan escape the **economic** problems of the worldwide depression.

Persecuting the Jews

The Austrian-born dictator of Germany, Adolf Hitler, believed that the German people were superior to all others. He also had a most vicious hatred for Jews. By 1935, laws in Germany had taken away Jews' citizenship, and later laws took away still more rights. Many German Jews tried to flee to other lands, but only a few succeeded. Once World War II began and German troops overran other nations, Hitler's followers killed many thousands of captured Jews. They drove tens of thousands into concentration camps. Eventually, the Nazis adopted what they called "the final solution to the Jewish problem." They set up "death camps" where they systematically killed people. In the end, the Nazis killed more than six million European Jews, an atrocity now called the Holocaust.

Jews in Warsaw, Poland, are captured by Nazi soldiers.

Germany invaded and took over the eastern European country of Czechoslovakia in 1938. This photograph shows Hitler's Elite Guard marching through Prague, Czechoslovakia, after the invasion.

Growing Unease

These dictators and military rulers all expanded their countries' armies and navies. While people around the world worried about this military expansion, nothing was done to stop them. In Europe, Britain and France faced their own problems of depression and unrest, and their leaders did not believe anyone would start a new war. In the United States, most Americans simply ignored events in Europe. They, too, worried more about their own shattered economy.

The dictators, meanwhile, began to move. In 1931, Japanese troops moved to take control of Manchuria, a part of China. Four years later, in 1935, Italian troops invaded Ethiopia, and Mussolini and Hitler signed a **treaty** of alliance. In 1937, Japanese troops pushed further into China, and Japan joined the alliance of Germany and Italy. In March 1938, Hitler took over Austria, and he seized Czechoslovakia later that year.

Still Britain and France did nothing. Leaders tried to reassure their people that by maintaining diplomatic relations, they could control Hitler and Mussolini.

A World War

In August 1939, the situation took a new, more sinister turn. Hitler signed a treaty with the Soviet Union. Hitler and Soviet leader Josef Stalin had been bitter enemies before; now they were on the same side. Between their large countries lay Poland, vulnerable because it had a much smaller army.

Britain and France promised to defend Poland's independence, but that did not stop Hitler. On September 1, 1939, German forces invaded Poland, and World War II had begun. Britain and France quickly declared war on Germany. The Germans were much better prepared for war, however, and their powerful army swept through Poland in just four weeks. In the spring of the next year, German forces moved west. They quickly took control of Denmark, the Netherlands, Norway, and Belgium. By July 1940, Germany had conquered France. Only Britain now stood against German power.

In 1940 and 1941, Hitler's airforce launched daily bombing attacks on Britain, preparing to invade it. The invasion never came—instead, in June of 1941, Hitler betrayed Stalin and sent his armies to attack the Soviet Union. The well-trained German forces overran the surprised Soviets and moved deep into Russia.

The United States Goes to War
Meanwhile, the U.S. involvement in the war was growing. Officially, the country took neither side. Still, President Franklin

As Europe fell into Nazi hands, Britain fought back by mass bombing German cities. In this photograph, citizens of Dresden in Germany try to board trams amidst the ruins left after a bombing raid.

In the devastating Japanese attack on Pearl Harbor, nearly 2,400 Americans were killed. Hundreds of planes and many ships, including the one in the center of this photograph, were destroyed in the attack.

Roosevelt saw Hitler and Japan as threats to the United States. He gave aid and supplies to Britain, China, and, after June 1941, the Soviet Union.

Late in 1941, the United States became a combatant. On December 7, the Japanese navy launched a surprise attack against the U.S. Navy base at Pearl Harbor in Hawaii. The next day, Congress declared war on Japan. Within days, Germany and the United States were formally at war as well.

The Allies and the Axis

The opponents were now defined. The United States, Britain, the Soviet Union, and many other nations were the **Allies.** They faced the **Axis**— Germany, Italy, Japan, and a few other countries.

At first the Axis gained the upper hand. The Japanese gained control of the Philippines, most of Southeast Asia, and parts of New Guinea. Meanwhile, the Germans were pushing farther into Soviet territory. They had also captured much of southeastern Europe and North Africa. Through much of 1942, the Allies were reeling.

Bitter Message

"With profound regret and with continued pride in my gallant men, I go to meet the Japanese commander. Good-bye, Mr. President."

General Jonathan Wainwright, message to President Roosevelt, before surrendering last U.S. troops in the Philippines, 1942

The Weapons of World War II

Conventional bombs were not as devastating as the atomic bomb, but they were responsible for hundreds of thousands of civilian deaths during World War II. The Allies used a strategy of mass bombing from airplanes—starting in 1942, the British bombed several German cities, and dozens of Japanese cities were badly damaged by U.S. fire bombings in the spring of 1945. The bombing of Tokyo alone left 125,000 casualties and destroyed 40 percent of the city.

Heavy armored tanks were the main offensive land weapon in invasions or

The V-1, shown here about to crash and explode in a British city in 1944, looked like an aircraft but had no pilot.

assaults, except in the jungles and islands of the Pacific, where they were impractical. In response, anti-tank weapons were used in large numbers—millions of landmines, laid in the ground to blow up tanks during World War II, remain buried in the deserts of North Africa today.

Guided missiles were a dangerous development—these long-range weapons, such as the German V-1, traveled through the air for a set distance and exploded when they crashed to the ground. The earliest **ballistic missiles** appeared in World War II, when the Germans began using V-2 rockets to carry bombs to enemy targets. At sea, submarines could attack and sink warships by firing torpedoes through the water.

Splitting the Atom

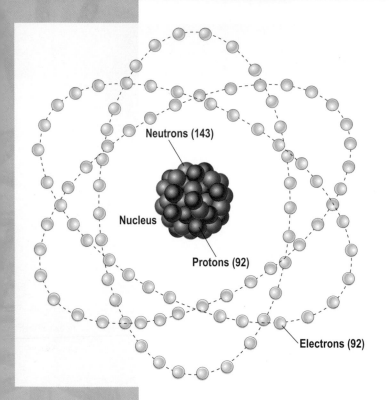

Neutrons (143)

Nucleus

Protons (92)

Electrons (92)

All atoms have a nucleus—comprising protons and neutrons—surrounded by electrons. This diagram shows the structure of an atom of a type of uranium called U-235, the element that is used to create nuclear energy.

Shaping Destiny

"If [the power of the atom] could be tapped and controlled what an agent it would be in shaping the world's destiny! The man who put his hand on the lever by which . . . nature regulates . . . this store of energy would possess a weapon by which he could destroy the earth."

Scientist Frederick Soddy, speaking in a lecture, 1904

As war spread across the globe, other developments were taking place on the scientific front. These developments were connected to World War II because scientists were researching atomic energy, something that had potential to provide the warring world with the most destructive weapon that it had ever known.

Atomic Theory

Before World War II, scientists were just beginning to understand the structure of **atoms,** the tiny bits of matter that make up every physical thing. By the 1930s, some things were known about atoms. Scientists saw them as miniature solar systems because all atoms have a central core, or nucleus, with electrons spinning around it. Physicists—scientists who work in the field of physics—had learned that electrons have a negative electrical charge. They also knew that the nucleus holds protons, which have a positive charge.

Scientists knew about ninety different **elements,** or basic substances. They also knew that some elements have **radioactivity.** In these elements, the nucleus is not stable but decays, or gives off bits

of matter. When that happens, the atoms also give off energy. British scientist Frederick Soddy suggested as early as 1904 that this reaction could be used to generate huge amounts of power.

Neutrons and Chain Reactions

In the 1930s, the structure of the atom and radioactivity still held many puzzles. In 1932, however, British scientist James Chadwick discovered another particle in the nucleus of an atom. He called it the neutron because it was neutral, having neither a positive nor a negative electrical charge.

Important atomic research was being carried on in many different countries, including Germany. Some of the scientists working there were Jewish, and they lost their jobs in 1933 because of Hitler's campaign against Jews. Many of these scientists began to flee the country, including physicist Leo Szilard, who went to Britain and continued his work there.

In London in 1933, Szilard had an important insight about neutrons when he realized that they could be sent through the electron "shell" of another atom and hit that atom's nucleus, causing it to give off energy. That nucleus could absorb the neutron but give off two or three more neutrons. Those neutrons could then go on and strike other atoms. This reaction would produce the same result—

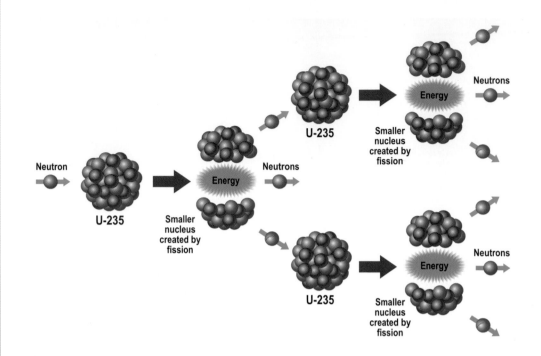

When a uranium atom is hit by a neutron, it causes the atom to split. Neutrons and energy are released, and the escaping neutrons split more atoms and create more energy. In a nuclear explosion, this reaction occurs billions of times in a fraction of a second.

each nucleus would pick up one neutron and give off some more. Those neutrons would have the same effect on yet more atoms. The result would be a **chain reaction**, an unbroken series of nuclear reactions that would release a huge amount of energy.

Leo Szilard (1898—1964)

Born in Hungary, Leo Szilard was a brilliant student. An idealist, he hoped to help bring peace to the world. Szilard studied physics in Berlin, Germany. He earned his doctorate with a creative solution to a difficult problem. He remained in Germany, teaching, but lost his job when the Nazis came to power—his background was Jewish. He settled in Britain, where he helped other Jewish scientists find jobs outside Germany, and then moved to the United States. Although he worked on the Manhattan Project, Szilard remained devoted to peace. After the successful atomic bomb test, he urged the government not to use the weapon. After the war, he worked to introduce international controls on nuclear weapons.

An Important Advance

Szilard's insight was soon demonstrated. In Italy in 1934, Enrico Fermi shot neutrons at atoms of uranium, an element with a large nucleus. The action produced new substances, although Fermi could not figure out what they were. Four years later, physicists in Germany did similar work and realized that they had produced two lighter elements. They had broken the uranium atom into smaller bits, a process named **nuclear fission.**

Scientists quickly saw the importance of this new discovery. If splitting these atoms released free neutrons, they could make the chain reaction Szilard had thought about earlier. And each time uranium atoms split, they should—as Soddy had seen—release large amounts of energy. Here was a source of power and also the potential for a very destructive weapon.

> "[These discoveries] might lead to a large-scale production of energy . . . [but] unfortunately also perhaps to atomic bombs. This new discovery revives all the hopes and fears in this respect which I had in 1934 and 1935."
>
> *Leo Szilard, letter to a friend, 1939*

Enrico Fermi (1901–1954)

Enrico Fermi was born and raised in Italy, where he earned his doctorate at the age of twenty-one and became a full professor at twenty-five. Fermi continued to teach and do important research. He and his wife were opponents of Mussolini, however, and became fearful when Italy passed anti-Jewish laws because Fermi's wife was Jewish. In 1938, when Fermi won the Nobel Prize in physics, he and his family traveled to Sweden to accept the award. They used the opportunity to flee to the United States, where Fermi later became an important part of the Manhattan Project. He taught and worked at the University of Chicago until his death.

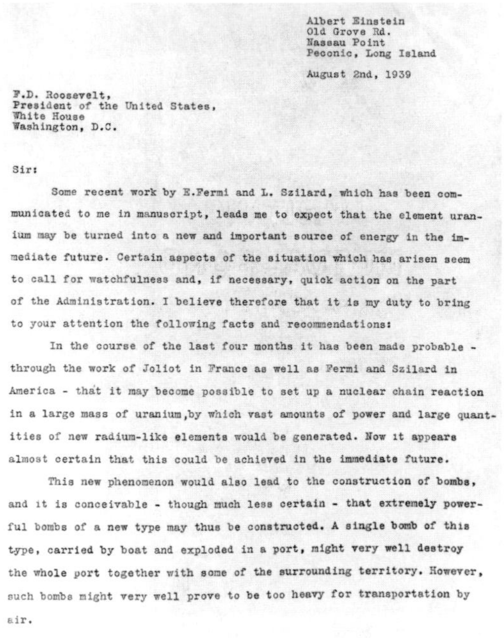

A two-page letter dated August 2, 1939, from Albert Einstein warned President Roosevelt that Germany was probably working on nuclear energy research. In the letter, Einstein advised of the possibilities and implications of such research.

Albert Einstein
Old Grove Rd.
Nassau Point
Peconic, Long Island

August 2nd, 1939

F.D. Roosevelt,
President of the United States,
White House
Washington, D.C.

Sir:

Some recent work by E.Fermi and L. Szilard, which has been communicated to me in manuscript, leads me to expect that the element uranium may be turned into a new and important source of energy in the immediate future. Certain aspects of the situation which has arisen seem to call for watchfulness and, if necessary, quick action on the part of the Administration. I believe therefore that it is my duty to bring to your attention the following facts and recommendations:

In the course of the last four months it has been made probable - through the work of Joliot in France as well as Fermi and Szilard in America - that it may become possible to set up a nuclear chain reaction in a large mass of uranium, by which vast amounts of power and large quantities of new radium-like elements would be generated. Now it appears almost certain that this could be achieved in the immediate future.

This new phenomenon would also lead to the construction of bombs, and it is conceivable - though much less certain - that extremely powerful bombs of a new type may thus be constructed. A single bomb of this type, carried by boat and exploded in a port, might very well destroy the whole port together with some of the surrounding territory. However, such bombs might very well prove to be too heavy for transportation by air.

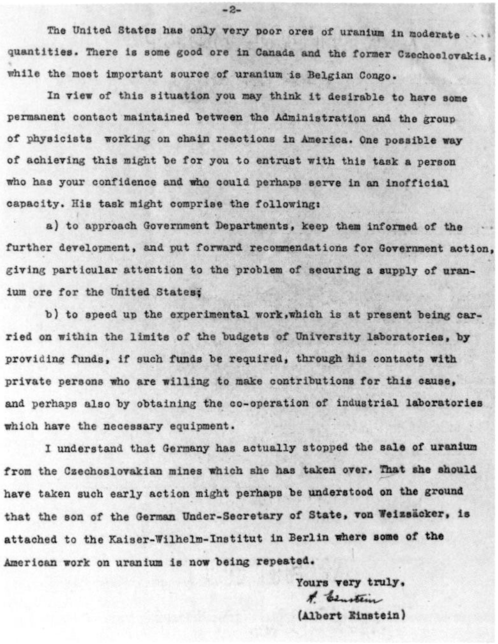

-2-

The United States has only very poor ores of uranium in moderate quantities. There is some good ore in Canada and the former Czechoslovakia, while the most important source of uranium is Belgian Congo.

In view of this situation you may think it desirable to have some permanent contact maintained between the Administration and the group of physicists working on chain reactions in America. One possible way of achieving this might be for you to entrust with this task a person who has your confidence and who could perhaps serve in an inofficial capacity. His task might comprise the following:

a) to approach Government Departments, keep them informed of the further development, and put forward recommendations for Government action, giving particular attention to the problem of securing a supply of uranium ore for the United States;

b) to speed up the experimental work, which is at present being carried on within the limits of the budgets of University laboratories, by providing funds, if such funds be required, through his contacts with private persons who are willing to make contributions for this cause, and perhaps also by obtaining the co-operation of industrial laboratories which have the necessary equipment.

I understand that Germany has actually stopped the sale of uranium from the Czechoslovakian mines which she has taken over. That she should have taken such early action might perhaps be understood on the ground that the son of the German Under-Secretary of State, von Weizsäcker, is attached to the Kaiser-Wilhelm-Institut in Berlin where some of the American work on uranium is now being repeated.

Yours very truly,

(Albert Einstein)

The Scientists Speak Out

In 1938, although World War II had not yet begun, storm clouds were gathering in Europe. Szilard worried what might happen if the new scientific knowledge came into the hands of Hitler or Mussolini. He talked over the problem with others who had escaped German persecution of the Jews. They decided that someone in power needed to know about this potential weapon, and therefore they needed a prominent person to deliver their message. They turned to Albert Einstein, whom Szilard had known from the University of Berlin. Einstein, the most famous physicist in the world, had also fled Germany in the early 1930s.

In the summer of 1939, Szilard explained the situation to Einstein, who quickly grasped the danger of the Germans making a nuclear weapon. Together with Alexander Sachs, an influential economist, they agreed that President Roosevelt was the person to approach. Sachs agreed to talk to the president, whom he knew.

Szilard and the others wrote a letter outlining the potential power of an atomic bomb, and Einstein signed it. In their letter, the scientists suggested that the president appoint someone to speed up experimental work in the area of nuclear weapons. They also suggested that the United States work to obtain a secure supply of uranium for this purpose. They ended the letter ominously, pointing out that the German government had stopped the sale of uranium from mines it controlled.

A Meeting with the President

The president could not meet with Sachs until two months after getting the letter. In the meantime, World War II had begun. Finally, on October 11, 1939, a meeting with the president took place. Sachs described to Roosevelt the concerns of the scientists and outlined the potential of nuclear power. Roosevelt said, "This requires action," and told an aide to take steps.

As a result, a government committee was set up and met a few days later. Officers from the army and navy who served on the committee scoffed at the scientists' talk of a bomb. Still, the members agreed to keep track of progress and to provide a small amount of money—just $6,000—to scientists working on the issue.

A Warning

"A single bomb of this type, carried by boat and exploded in a port, might very well destroy the whole port [city] together with some of the surrounding territory."

Albert Einstein, letter to President Franklin Roosevelt, August 2, 1939

This photograph of President Franklin D. Roosevelt in his office at the White House was taken in 1945, not long before he died. After the president's meeting with Alexander Sachs in 1939, the government began to provide funds for nuclear research.

Chapter 3

The Manhattan Project

The First Obstacle

Many obstacles stood in the way of developing an atomic bomb. The first was getting enough **fissionable material** to make a bomb. Scientists knew they could use uranium, but the United States did not have a supply of uranium ore. After 1941, plutonium became another possible material. It was a new element, first made in 1941 by adding particles of **deuteron** to uranium. There was not enough of it to make a bomb, however—all the plutonium in the world was smaller than a period on this page.

There were other problems, too. Scientists did not know how much material they would need to make a bomb. They did not know if such a **critical mass** would be small enough that it could be easily moved, as a bomb must be. Nor did they know how to make sure such a bomb did not go off too early.

When the U.S. nuclear program began, the United States did not know that there were huge uranium deposits in New Mexico. From 1950, this mine near Grants, New Mexico, produced thousands of tons of uranium ore every day.

An important part of the Manhattan Project was based at Oak Ridge, Tennessee, where huge plants were built for processing uranium.

Processing the Elements

In addition, the scientists would have to figure out how to make the bomb without being able to test their ideas. Months were needed to get the uranium and plutonium. Indeed, months were needed to build the huge plants needed to process those elements because no such facilities existed. They could not be built right away, either, because scientists did not know the best method to use to process the elements. Uranium has two forms, but almost all raw uranium is of the form that cannot be used in a bomb. Scientists did not

Finding a Uranium Supply

The problem of uranium supply was solved by 1942, when a mining company in Canada agreed to sell large amounts of the now-important metal. The mine had been shut down, however, and the company would need time to reopen it and begin mining the metal. Fortunately, the government learned of a supply of uranium sitting in a New York warehouse. This metal had been shipped out of Africa—where World War II was raging—by a Belgian mine owner to prevent it from falling into Hitler's hands.

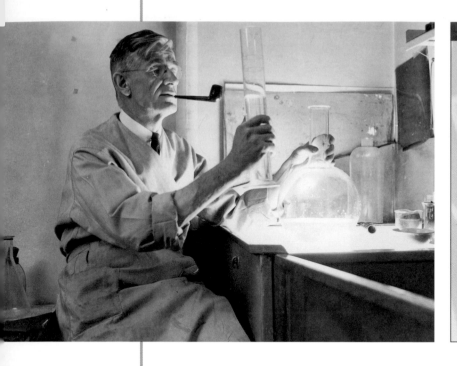

As head of the Office of Scientific Research and Development, electrical engineer Dr. Vannevar Bush was the link between government and the work of thousands of U.S. scientists in the nation's war effort. After the war, Bush's ideas about linking and storing information influenced the development, years later, of the Internet.

know how to separate out the right type without huge expense. Nor did they have a good way to make plutonium in large amounts.

Encouraging Words

Some of the first obstacles began to drop away quickly as more research was done. The British government had formed a committee of top scientists, code-named MAUD, to study the possibility of building a bomb. In July 1941, MAUD issued its report.

The British scientists said they were convinced that a small enough amount of uranium could be used to make a bomb that could be dropped by an airplane. They addressed several other issues, including how to process the uranium, how to set off an explosion, and how large the explosion would be. The report was very promising, and they urged that more work be carried out.

"OK"

News of the British report reached Dr. Vannevar Bush, President Roosevelt's advisor on scientific matters. Bush had had some doubts about the possibility of a uranium bomb before, but the British report changed his mind. He had a separate report written to give Roosevelt. It, too, said that it was possible to build a transportable atomic bomb. The report concluded that "if all possible effort is spent on the program, fission bombs [might] be available in three or four years." The president returned it with the answer: "OK."

In December of 1941, Bush took charge of coordinating the atomic research. He named leading scientists at three universities—the University of Chicago, University of California at Berkeley, and Columbia in New York City—to oversee key research.

Success in Chicago

One area of research was being performed by Enrico Fermi at the University of Chicago. His job was to create a controlled chain reaction. He and his crew had to put together a mass of uranium—called a pile—and hit it with enough neutrons to cause fission. But they had to make sure the reaction was not so strong that the pile exploded or gave off dangerous levels of radioactivity.

They built the pile in an unused squash court beneath a stadium at the university. To control the reaction they built a frame of pure graphite rods around each lump of uranium. Some of the rods, called control rods, could be moved into and out of the pile. Taking them out allowed the reaction to take place, and putting them back stopped the reaction.

Enrico Fermi's work at the University of Chicago was vital to the development of the atom bomb and later nuclear energy research. This machine, displayed by Fermi's team at the University of Chicago after the war, was a 450-million-volt synchrocyclotron, also called an "atom-smasher."

Fermi's team worked around the clock in two twelve-hour shifts to build the pile. On December 2, 1942, it was ready to test. The morning's experiment failed, but Fermi calmly told his team to have lunch and try again in the afternoon. The second attempt was a complete success. When the graphite control rods were taken out, a chain reaction took place. After a few minutes, Fermi had the rods put back in to stop the chain reaction.

New Man in Charge

By the time of Fermi's experiment, the whole research effort had been placed under the control of the U.S. Army. Overall command was given to an officer named Leslie Groves. He was in charge of the research, the building of new facilities, the security, and the building of any weapons.

Leslie Groves (1898—1970)

Born in Albany, New York, Leslie Groves was the son of an army chaplain. He had three years of university before studying at the U.S. Military Academy, from which he graduated in 1918. As part of the Army Corps of Engineers, Groves took part in many construction projects. By 1941, he was overseeing the building of the Pentagon, the new headquarters for the U.S. War Department and the world's largest office building.

Full of energy and willing to make decisions, Groves could also be gruff. He sometimes annoyed the scientists in the Manhattan Project, whom he viewed as "prima donnas," and he sometimes angered other military personnel. "I hated his guts and so did everybody else," a junior officer recalled.

After the war, Groves oversaw atomic weapons research for two more years. In 1948, he retired from the service and for the next thirteen years worked for a private corporation.

Within days of taking charge, Groves did three important things. He ordered the purchase of the Belgian-owned uranium that was stored in New York. He authorized the purchase of a large chunk of land in Tennessee, where a plant to process uranium would be built. And he worked within the army to get the project a top priority rating so that requests for supplies would be handled as fast as possible.

J. Robert Oppenheimer was working at the University of California at Berkeley when he was recruited by Major General Leslie Groves to direct the Manhattan Project laboratory. Some people doubted his abilities and his loyalty, but Groves' choice was justified when Oppenheimer turned out to be a powerful leader as well as a gifted scientist.

Assembling a Team

Groves traveled to the different research sites to talk to the scientists about their work. On a California trip, he met physicist J. Robert Oppenheimer, who told Groves that the project needed a central laboratory. There, said Oppenheimer, scientists with many different specialties could work together to carry out the complex work of designing an atomic bomb.

Groves agreed and quickly settled on Oppenheimer to lead the central lab. Everyone did not agree on this choice. The scientist had never led such an effort, and some colleagues thought he did not know enough about experiments—he was more of a theorist. Security people worried because some members of Oppenheimer's family had been communists. The security officers feared he would

The Man for the Job

"I knew . . . that he was a man of tremendous intellectual capacity. . . . I thought he could do the job. In all my inquiries, I was unable to find anyone else who was available who I felt would do as well."

General Leslie Groves, recalling why he wanted Oppenheimer, 1962

In spite of its name, the Manhattan Project did not take place in Manhattan, although some initial research was done at Columbia University in New York City. This map shows the key sites of the Manhattan Project around the United States.

give military secrets to the Soviet Union. Groves insisted, however, and got his man.

Oppenheimer began recruiting other scientists. Some did not want to disrupt their lives, and others were involved in different research for the war that they thought equally important. Still, he managed to grab many of the top physicists of the day.

Naming the Manhattan Project

How did the atomic bomb program come to be named the "Manhattan Project" when none of the work took place in Manhattan? The seed of the name was planted before General Groves took charge, when an army engineer was first named to coordinate the work being done on atomic research. Since his office had been in Manhattan in New York City, the work was called the Manhattan Engineering District. This followed naming traditions used by army engineers. It was also good for security—the name did not reveal anything about the important work being done. Later, the work was simply called the Manhattan Project.

General Leslie Groves (center, seated) looks over a map with members of the Manhattan Project's Technical Board. Military personnel and scientists had to work together on the project, and they didn't always get along so well.

Following Many Leads

By the end of 1942, much had been accomplished, and the Manhattan Project—as it was called—was well underway. A key early decision was to follow as many leads as possible. Gaining success meant trying everything, even if that meant some ideas would turn out to be dead ends. Only by trying and failing, Groves reasoned, could that be known.

Of course, trying more than one method added to the cost of the project. Back in 1939, the government had first committed to giving the scientists only $6,000. By 1945, the cost of the project had reached $2 billion and was still going up.

Build Both

"There is no objection to a wrong decision that produces quick results. If there is a choice between two methods, one of which is good and the other looks promising, then build both."

General Leslie Groves, talking to University of Chicago team, 1942

Chapter 4

At Los Alamos

This building at the Hanford Nuclear Reservation in Washington housed a nuclear reactor built for the Manhattan Project. The Hanford facility manufactured the plutonium that was used in the atom bomb test and in the bomb dropped on Nagasaki, Japan.

Many Locations

For the project to work, Groves needed to build several different facilities. Near Knoxville, Tennessee, plants were built to process uranium and plutonium. The plutonium-producing plant, though, was too small to make enough of that material. As a result, a larger plant was built in a remote desert area in western Washington state. The third major facility was the scientists' laboratory. It was placed in north central New Mexico at a spot called Los Alamos.

The Tennessee and Washington plants had to be built from scratch. Both needed housing for the workers—even for the construction workers who built the plants. Los Alamos also needed housing, power and phone lines, and streets.

The project had other sites as well. Research was carrying on at Berkeley, California, and Chicago. Groves's main office was in Washington, D.C., and in Santa Fe, New Mexico, there was an office where people going to Los Alamos stopped. Dorothy McKibbin headed this office, greeting the scientists and getting them, their families, and their belongings on their way to the laboratory.

Overcoming Difficulties

Workers in Tennessee tried to discover the best ways to process the materials. They settled on two methods. One involved combining uranium with a gas and passing it through thousands of miles of pipes and filters. The other used huge magnets. In Washington state, the new Hanford plant housed a larger version of Fermi's

How Los Alamos Was Chosen

The scientific research was placed at Los Alamos for several reasons. The army wanted a place that was large enough for all the people and facilities. It had to be far from any communities to prevent spying—or endangering people if an accident occurred. And it had to be easy to make secure.

An aide to Groves suggested a spot in New Mexico. When Oppenheimer saw it, he objected because the valley did not have the gorgeous scenery

The lodge at Los Alamos before the Manhattan Project took over the property.

typical of the Southwest. He suggested nearby Los Alamos Ranch, a boarding school near Santa Fe that he knew of from childhood visits to the area. When Groves saw it, he approved Los Alamos immediately. The government bought the school and surrounding land and took over the site early in 1943.

uranium pile. At Hanford, scientists caused chain reactions and also manufactured plutonium.

By late 1944, Tennessee was churning out larger and larger amounts of uranium. Plutonium began arriving at Los Alamos in small amounts late in 1943. By 1944, the Washington site was sending larger supplies.

Meanwhile, the scientists at Los Alamos solved another of their problems—how to turn the material they got into a form pure enough to use in a bomb. Without uranium or plutonium at first, they tested their ideas successfully on other metals.

Secrecy

All workers followed the utmost secrecy. The government worried that the Germans might learn about any progress and use the information to further their own efforts. There was also concern that American communists might tell the Soviet Union about advances. Although that country was a U.S. ally in the war, many people did not trust its communist regime.

There were many obvious signs of security concerns. The scientists all needed security clearances before joining the project.

Main Street, Los Alamos, pictured here, sprang up in 1943 in the mountains of northern New Mexico. Nobody who worked there was allowed to talk about the project.

People and places were given code names. Soldiers patrolled the major sites. Barbed wire surrounded Los Alamos. Workers were forbidden to discuss their work with anyone outside the project. Telephone calls were listened to, and letters were opened and read.

Many were not entirely happy about these rules. One scientist recalled, "I couldn't go to Santa Fe without being aware of hidden eyes upon me, watching. . . . It wasn't a pleasant feeling."

A major source of anger was the policy of compartmentalization. Groves felt that security would be stronger if people did not know more than they needed to know. The more information that was shared, he feared, the more was likely to leak out. Scientists working on one part of the project, then, should not have information about another part. This went directly against the way the scientists liked to work. They wanted a free flow of ideas, a sharing of views that could sometimes help them solve problems. They argued that Groves's policy slowed down progress.

In the fall of 1945, the first outsiders were allowed to visit Los Alamos to see how 6,000 people lived in the formerly secret community. A newspaper photographer took this picture of the one-family houses that had been hastily built during the war.

J. Robert Oppenheimer (1904—1967)

The son of a German immigrant to the United States, Robert Oppenheimer studied science, languages, and philosophy at Harvard University. Oppenheimer then studied with some of the world's top atomic scientists in both Britain and Germany. He earned his doctorate in Germany in 1927 and two years later returned to the United States to teach.

Robert Oppenheimer (left, in hat) received a military award from General Groves (center, in uniform) after the Manhattan Project was over.

Concern about Mussolini and Hitler led Oppenheimer to send money to groups, some linked to communists, who opposed these dictators. He never joined the Communist party, but these actions raised questions about him. Groves, however, trusted Oppenheimer's loyalty completely.

Oppenheimer worried deeply about the potential of the atomic bomb once it had been used. In late 1945, he resigned as director of Los Alamos, although he continued to serve as a government advisor. He opposed development of the even more powerful hydrogen bomb. In 1953, some in the government questioned his loyalty to the United States. A hearing found him not guilty of treason but recommended he no longer be allowed to know secrets about nuclear weapons. Many scientists protested the decision. In 1963, President Lyndon Johnson made up for this treatment by giving Oppenheimer a top award for nuclear research.

Enrico Fermi (right) on a hike with other Manhattan Project workers in the mountains around the Los Alamos laboratory.

Tension on the Team

Work on the project was stressful, and there was often tension. Military officers and the scientists often did not see eye to eye. There were also disagreements among the scientists themselves. Some were based on personal rivalries. Some had political roots. Through all the disagreements and pressures, Oppenheimer—known as "Oppie"—kept the scientists working together and focused on their tasks.

Taking a Break

The scientists at Los Alamos worked long hours, typically six days a week. On Saturday nights and Sundays, they relaxed. Some enjoyed square dancing; others staged plays. Once there was a mock ballet that poked fun at Groves, Oppenheimer, and others. The army had a store of movies to show, and some of the scientists played poker on Saturday nights. Others took the time to learn how to play a musical instrument.

Many spent their Sundays in outdoor recreation. Oppenheimer and his wife often went horseback riding, an activity he had enjoyed as a child. Others went fishing or hiking in the beautiful rocky landscape in which they lived.

31

The Trinity Test

Two Kinds of Explosion

The Los Alamos team struggled with a key issue—how to make an atomic bomb explode. They had two ideas. The "gun method" involved having two chunks of material that together made a critical mass, but separately did not. By shooting one into the other, the scientists thought they could create a critical mass and cause a chain reaction. The other was the **implosion** method. In this, a small mass of material would be surrounded with ordinary explosives. When the explosives were detonated, the blast would push against the nuclear fuel, forcing it into less space. Compressing it in this way would turn the matter into a critical mass and cause a chain reaction.

The gun system was favored. It worked in a way similar to the way traditional weapons work. In 1944, however, it became clear that this system would not work with a plutonium bomb, which needed the implosion method. As a result, work continued on both types of

The U.S. Department of Defense released this photograph of a Little Boy bomb in 1960. The ten-foot (3-m) long bomb was the type dropped on Hiroshima in 1945.

Fat Man and Little Boy

Workers on the Manhattan Project used code-names to hide the fact that they were working on weapons. In case messages were intercepted, they called the thinner gun bomb "Thin Man" and the wider implosion bomb "Fat Man." Eventually, scientists found they could make the gun bomb smaller. This replacement for Thin Man was dubbed "Little Boy."

bomb, a plutonium implosion bomb called "Fat Man" and a gun method bomb using uranium that was named "Little Boy." The scientists worked toward testing their two bomb designs.

Testing Little Boy

One group worked on testing the gun method to be used for Little Boy. The scientists would assemble a mass of uranium not large enough to reach a chain reaction. Then they would drop enough

The Fat Man bomb sits ready to be detonated at the test site in New Mexico in 1945. Fat Man was the type of bomb dropped on Nagasaki in 1945.

At the Trinity Site, Manhattan Project workers built a tall tower in which the atomic bomb would be placed for testing.

new material into the center to produce the desired reaction. Since this test would not be done with pure metal, they believed—or hoped—it would create the reaction but not explode. On April 12, 1945, they did the test, and it was successful. The test proved that, when armed with pure uranium, the Little Boy method would create an atomic explosion.

The Trinity Site

The scientists at Los Alamos worried more about testing the implosion bomb, Fat Man, because it would involve an actual atomic explosion. Early in 1944, planning for the test began. The testing of Fat Man was given the code name Trinity, and a site was chosen for the test. The Trinity Site was on a remote area of army land, 200 miles (320 km) south of

Most Satisfactory

"It was as near as we could possibly go towards starting an atomic explosion without actually being blown up, and the results were most satisfactory. Everything happened exactly as it should."

Otto Frisch, Manhattan Project scientist, recalling the Little Boy test, 1979

Los Alamos, named the *Jornada del Muerto*—the "Journey of Death." The name was fitting for a place to try out the world's most destructive weapon.

The Trinity Site soon had a base camp, 10 miles (16 km) from where the bomb would be tested. Base camp was where the scientists and support staff lived while they worked to prepare for the test. From the fall of 1944 through the spring of 1945, people

Setting Up the Test

One early step in preparing for the Trinity test was to blow up 100 tons of the explosive TNT, creating a huge blast that would approximate what the test bomb might produce. This trial, which took place on May 7, 1945, was needed to practice the countdown and test instruments. The explosion, close to the spot chosen for the atomic test, left a crater in the ground.

On July 12, the supply

Workers prepare to hoist the bomb to the top of the tower.

of plutonium that would be used for the bomb was taken to a ranch house, two miles (3.2 km) from the Trinity Site, which had been chosen as the place to assemble the bomb's core. At the Trinity Site, meanwhile, a 100-foot (30-meter) steel tower had been constructed. At the top was a small shelter in which the bomb would be placed. On July 13, first the explosives and then the plutonium core arrived at the Trinity Site, and the bomb was assembled under the tower. The next morning, July 14, the assembled bomb was raised to the top of the tower, and the detonators—which would set off the explosion of the TNT—were attached. The bomb was ready to be tested.

continued to arrive at the Trinity base camp to work in secrecy on the project. Work for the test continued at Los Alamos, too.

Throughout early 1945, members of the project worked feverishly, putting in long hours every day and getting little sleep. As the months passed, the scientists felt more and more pressure. The test was set for July 16, 1945. In the weeks before the Trinity test, the tension became severe.

The Test

At 4:00 A.M. on July 16, scientists and soldiers gathered at three observation points, which were shelters about 5.5 miles (about 9 km) from "ground zero," the spot where the test bomb sat at the top

A photograph of base camp shows some of the temporary buildings in which scientists lived and worked in 1944–1945. All the buildings shown here were removed after the test.

of the tower. One of the observation points was also the control center—it was from there that the bomb was triggered and the key scientists watched and directed operations.

At their observation points, the spectators clustered in wooden shelters protected by concrete and dirt. "With the darkness and the waiting in the chill of the desert the tension became almost unendurable," one later recalled. Others, including General Groves, watched from the Trinity base camp ten miles (16 km) away. A group of important visitors watched from 20 miles (32 km) away.

Just before 5:10 A.M., the countdown began. At 5:29 and 45 seconds, the bomb exploded in a blinding flash of light, a light so strong, one scientist wrote, that "it bored its way right through you." It was followed by a ball of fire that reached 2,000 feet (600 m) across. The heat was so intense it could be felt nearly 11 miles (18 km) away. The blast had the force of nearly 20,000 tons of dynamite. "It worked," Oppenheimer said.

At ground zero, the heat of the blast melted the tower and the sand around it, but left only a shallow crater. The shock waves from the explosions, however, had a huge impact, breaking windows over 100 miles (160 km) away. To explain this, the U.S. Army announced to the public that an explosives store had accidentally blown up.

This series of photographs captured the bomb blast at 0.016 seconds (top), 4 seconds (center), and 20 seconds (bottom) after the Trinity bomb exploded.

Chapter 6

Dropping the Bomb

A wounded Marine is given blood plasma by a medic after being wounded on Okinawa, a Japanese island that saw some of the Pacific's worst fighting in World War II.

Progress of the War

By the time of the Trinity test, the war situation had changed dramatically. The Allies had turned the tide of war in Europe. In May 1945, Germany surrendered, and there was no longer a need to fear the Germans developing an atomic bomb.

The war in the Pacific continued and escalated. U.S. troops had gained much ground, and Japanese forces were being pushed back toward Japan. They were fighting fiercely, however, and American casualties were climbing.

Civilian casualties were mounting in Japan as well. In the spring of 1945, U.S. planes began low-level bombing raids over Japanese cities that killed tens of thousands of people. Still, Japan's government refused to surrender. U.S. military commanders began planning to invade Japan, but they feared the cost in life. Some said that hundreds of thousands of American troops would be killed, and 2 million Japanese might die as well. To some in power, it was beginning to seem that there was no way to end the Pacific war except by using the atomic bomb.

Intense Debate

Facing that terrible decision was a new president. On April 12—the same day that Little Boy was successfully tested—Franklin Roosevelt died, and Harry S. Truman became president of the United States. Within a few days, he was briefed in detail, for the first time, about the work of the Manhattan Project. Truman put together a committee of government leaders and scientists to discuss the options and make recommendations.

The group met on May 31 and June 1, 1945, and discussed several issues. They talked about whether the bomb should be used or not. They argued over whether a test should be made in front of Japanese observers, demonstrating the bomb's power without dropping it on a city. They discussed whether Truman should warn Japan of the power of the bomb and then demand surrender.

In the end, the group decided that a test was not a good idea, in case it did not work. They recommended that the bomb be dropped on a Japanese city that was a legitimate military target.

A Demand for Surrender

Truman, meanwhile, had a conference in July, in Potsdam, Germany, with the British and Soviet leaders. The Trinity test took

From July 17 to August 2, 1945, President Truman (center) attended the Potsdam Conference in Germany, where he met British prime minister Winston Churchill (left) and Soviet premier Josef Stalin (right). The conference's main purpose was to discuss postwar Europe, but on July 26, the leaders issued a joint ultimatum to Japan to surrender or face destruction.

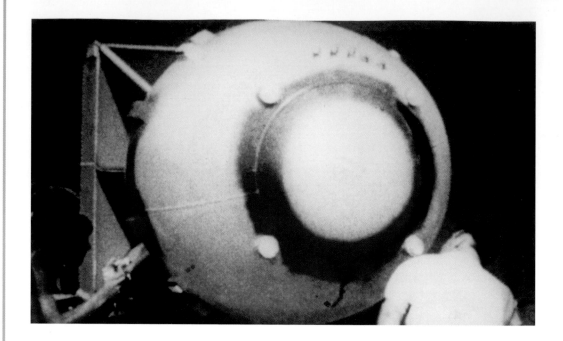

On the Pacific island of Tinian in the summer of 1945, a Fat Man bomb has been assembled and is being sealed in preparation for its mission.

place during the meeting, and Groves quickly sent a report of its success. Late in July, Truman agreed to drop the bomb any time after August 1 that weather permitted, unless the Japanese surrendered first. On July 26, the United States, Britain, and the Soviet Union issued a demand that Japan surrender.

After the successful tests, the teams had quickly built new atomic bombs of each type. On the day that the Allies demanded Japan's surrender, Little Boy and Fat Man, in pieces, were flown to an air base in the Pacific and assembled.

Using the Bomb

The Japanese did not surrender. On August 6, a U.S. bomber airplane named the *Enola Gay* set out from its base on Tinian Island in the western Pacific carrying Little Boy. Its target was Hiroshima, an industrial city in southern Japan with a population of about 250,000 people.

The blast was devastating, terrorizing the people of the city. Nearly everyone near where the bomb struck died. So did many more—somewhere between 70,000 and 80,000 were killed in all. Another 70,000 were hurt, and thousands more were traumatized by the horror of the charred bodies and the agonized faces of the people they saw. The city itself suffered when the intense fires destroyed all buildings in a four-square-mile (10-square-kilometer) area around the impact point.

Some members of Japan's government had been urging peace for months. Their pleas increased after Hiroshima, but some military leaders refused to surrender.

Three days later, the United States struck again. On August 9, Fat Man was dropped on the industrial city of Nagasaki, which had a population of about 200,000. This bomb killed another 35,000 to 40,000 people and injured just as many. Soon after the attack on Nagasaki, the Japanese surrendered. The war in the Pacific was finally over.

In both cities, the deaths continued for many months. Thousands more died by the end of 1945. Even more died in the next five years, sickened by **radiation** or succumbing to their burns. One estimate said that more than half the population of both cities died within five years.

A cloud of smoke, thousands of feet high, followed the explosion of the atomic bomb dropped on Nagasaki on August 9, 1945. On the ground below, thousands of people died instantly.

Conclusion

Los Alamos Today

The Los Alamos National Laboratory in New Mexico is today one of the largest government laboratories in the world. It is part of the National Nuclear Security Administration that oversees the U.S. nuclear weapons program. Managed by the University of California, Los Alamos employs over ten thousand people, many of them scientists.

At the U.S. Army's White Sands Missile Range nearby, the Trinity site where the first atomic bomb was exploded has been preserved as a national historic landmark. It is open to the public twice a year.

A Debate

The Manhattan Project was a success, but should the atomic bombs it developed have been used? Some

An aerial view of part of the Los Alamos National Laboratory, now run by the University of California for the Department of Energy's National Nuclear Security Administration.

Today, an obelisk (center) marks the exact spot of the Trinity test. The blue shelter in the background covers part of the ground to preserve it as it was right after the explosion. Under the shelter is a green, glasslike substance—called "trinitite"—that formed after the blast melted the sand around ground zero.

argue that doing so spared lives because an invasion of Japan would have resulted in many more casualties. Others say that the killing of civilians was immoral and cannot be justified.

Would the world be free of nuclear weapons if the Manhattan Project had never happened? Probably not. Others would probably have developed these weapons anyway. Would the world be better off if there had been no Manhattan Project? Perhaps not. The destruction it caused might mean some good for humankind. Hiroshima and Nagasaki stand as stark reminders of the massive death that atomic weapons bring. No one can even consider using them again without thinking of that.

The Legacy of the Atom Bomb Project

The Manhattan Project served as a model for the close cooperation of government and scientists. This kind of cooperation has been repeated several times since World War II—the space program and AIDS research are just two examples.

The main legacy of the development of the atom bomb, however, is the danger that nuclear weapons pose. For years, people all over the world have lived under the threat of possible nuclear war or nuclear attacks. The spread of nuclear weapons remains a major problem. Today, a great worry is that terrorists might obtain nuclear material and use it to attack innocent people.

Time Line

1922 ■ Benito Mussolini takes power in Italy.
1932 ■ Neutron is discovered.
1933 ■ Adolf Hitler takes power in Germany.
Leo Szilard develops theory of creating nuclear reaction by shooting neutrons at atoms.
1934 ■ Enrico Fermi demonstrates Szilard's theory with uranium, creating unidentified nuclear reaction.
1935 ■ German laws strip Jews of their citizenship.
Germany and Italy sign treaty of alliance.
1937 ■ Japan becomes ally of Germany and Italy.
1938 ■ German scientists split uranium atom.
1939 ■ August: Letter sent to President Roosevelt from group of scientists represented by Albert Einstein.
September: Germany invades Poland, and World War II begins.
October: Alexander Sachs meets President Roosevelt to discuss atomic weapons.
1941 ■ February: California researchers discover plutonium.
June: Germany invades Soviet Union.
July: British report offers encouragement on building atomic bomb.
December: President Roosevelt approves research into atomic weapons.
United States enters World War II.
1942 ■ September 23: Leslie Groves is put in charge of Manhattan Project.
December 2: Enrico Fermi succeeds in making a controlled chain reaction.
1943 ■ March: Scientists begin arriving at Los Alamos laboratory in New Mexico.
1945 ■ April 12: Successful test of Little Boy chain reaction takes place.
President Roosevelt dies, and Harry S. Truman becomes president.
May 7: Trinity trial run is made with conventional explosives.
Germany surrenders to Allies.
June 1: government committee recommends using atomic bomb on Japan.
July 16: Trinity test of Fat Man takes place.
July 24: Truman authorizes use of atomic bomb on Japan.
July 26: Potsdam Conference issues surrender demand to Japan.
August 6: Little Boy is dropped on Hiroshima.
August 9: Fat Man is dropped on Nagasaki.
August 14: Japan surrenders to Allies and World War II ends.

Glossary

Allies: name during World War II for the United States, Canada, Britain, and other nations fighting on the same side.

atom: tiny piece of matter making up everything in the physical world.

atomic: having to do with atoms; or based on the properties of atoms.

Axis: name during World War II for Germany, Italy, Japan, and a few other nations fighting against the Allies.

ballistic missile: explosive with its own system of power that carries it to its target.

chain reaction: continuing series of nuclear fissions.

civilian: person who is not a member of the armed forces.

communist: person who follows the principles of communism, a political system in which government owns and runs the nation's economy and has a lot of control over society. The Soviet Union was a communist nation.

critical mass: amount of fissionable material needed to have a chain reaction.

depression: breakdown of a nation's economy, when many businesses close and people lose their jobs.

deuteron: nucleus of a particular kind of hydrogen atom, which has one neutron and one proton. Deuteron combined with uranium produces plutonium.

economic: having to do with the economy, which is the system of producing and distributing goods and services.

element: one of the basic substances found in the world, such as oxygen, hydrogen, and carbon.

fascist: person who follows the principles of fascism, a system in which a government, often led by a dictator, has complete power over its citizens.

fissionable material: element that can be broken up by nuclear fission.

implosion: violent and sudden collapse inward of a mass of material; in an explosion, a mass goes outward.

nuclear energy: power given off by nuclear fission.

nuclear fission: process of splitting—or fission—of a nucleus by hitting it with particles; also called splitting the atom.

radiation: energy given off by radioactive elements.

radioactivity: characteristic of some elements, in which the nucleus decays, or gives off bits of matter. Some radiation can be dangerous to living things.

Soviet Union: former federation of communist states in eastern Europe and Asia. It was formed in 1917 and broke up in 1991.

treaty: agreement among two or more people or nations made after negotiation, often at the end of a period of conflict.

Further Information

Books

Egendorf, Laura L., ed. *Harry S. Truman* (Presidents and Their Decisions). Greenhaven Press, 2001.

Rummel, Jack. *Robert Oppenheimer: Dark Prince* (Makers of Modern Science). Facts On File, 1992.

Sheehan, Sean. *The Technology of World War II* (The World Wars). Raintree/Steck Vaughn, 2003.

Sherrow, Victoria. *The Making of the Atom Bomb* (World History). Lucent, 2000.

Streissguth, Thomas. *Nuclear Weapons: More Countries, More Threats* (Issues in Focus). Springfield, N.J.: Enslow, 2000.

Young, Robert. *Hiroshima: Fifty Years of Debate* (Both Sides). Dillon, 1994.

Web Sites

www.atomicarchive.com/librarymenu.shtml Background information on the people of the Manhattan Project and the events of the time; includes documents.

www.atomicmuseum.com Information about the Manhattan Project and other issues related to nuclear weapons from the National Atomic Museum.

www.wsmr.army.mil/paopage/Pages/trinph.htm U.S. Army web site for White Sands Missile Range offers information about the Trinity test and the Trinity Site today.

Useful Addresses

White Sands Missile Range
Public Affairs Office
Building 1782
White Sands, NM 88002
Telephone: (505) 678-1134

Index

Page numbers in *italics* indicate maps and diagrams. Page numbers in **bold** indicate other illustrations.